Barbara Perry

TROPICAL TREES & SHRUBS PLANTING
A Practical Guide

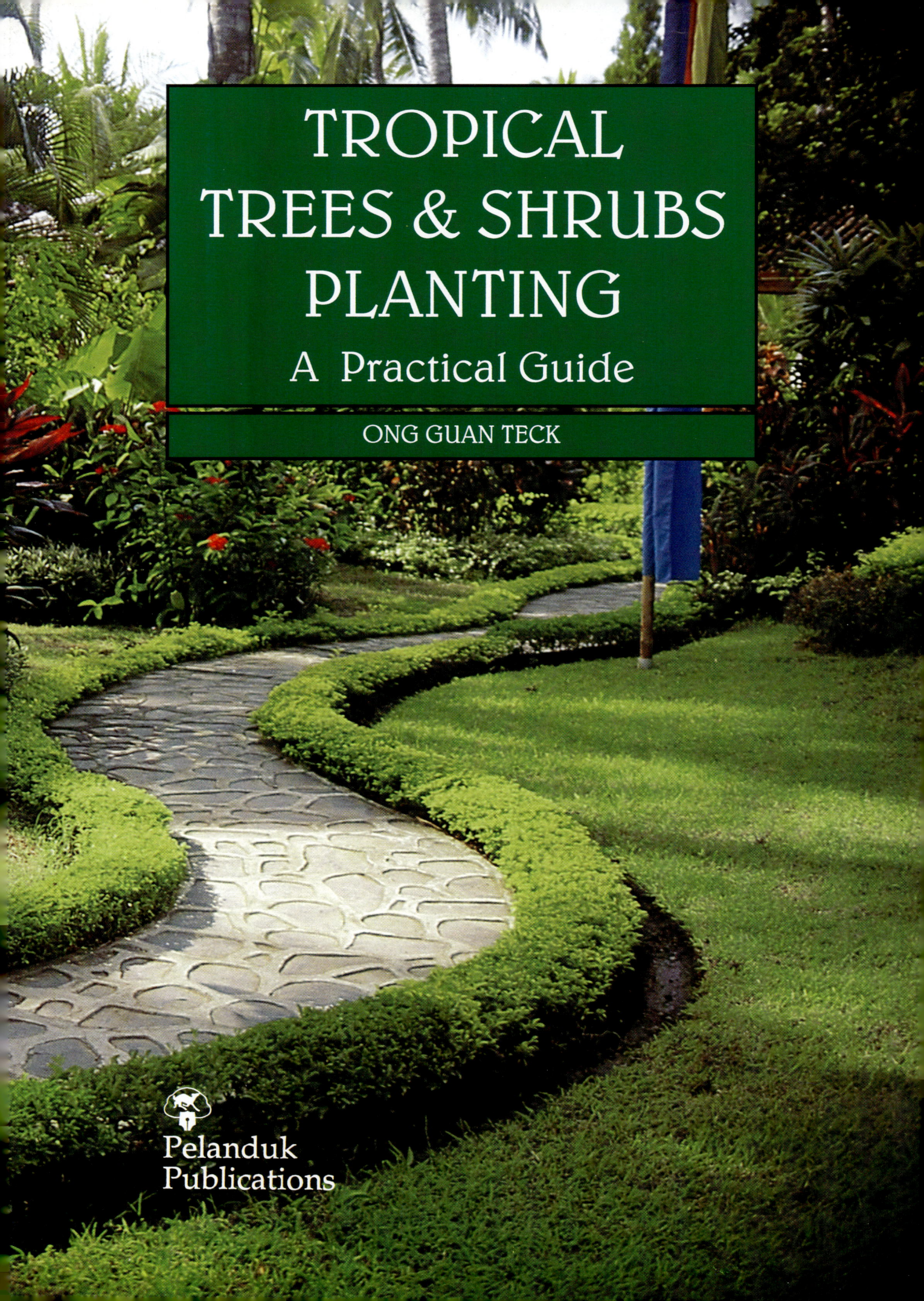

Published by
Pelanduk Publications (M) Sdn Bhd
(Co. No. 113307-W)
24 Jalan 20/16A 46300 Petaling Jaya,
Selangor Darul Ehsan, Malaysia.

Address all correspondence to
Pelanduk Publications (M) Sdn Bhd
P.O. Box 8265, 46785 Kelana Jaya,
Selangor Darul Ehsan, Malaysia.

Copyright © 1997 Ong Guan Teck.
Layout Design © 1997 Pelanduk Publications (M) Sdn Bhd.
Frontispiece © AT/Picture Library.

All rights reserved. No part of this book may be reproduced in any form or by any means without prior permission from the Publisher.

Perpustakaan Negara Malaysia Cataloguing-in-Publication Data

Ong, Guan Teck
    Tropical trees & shrubs planting: a practical guide / Ong Guan Teck.
    ISBN 967-978-611-0
    1. Ornamental woody plants. 2. Landscape plants. 3. Landscape gardening. I. Title.
    715

Printed by Academe Art & Printing Services Sdn. Bhd.

Foreword

"Trees and a more liveable world!" A statement not many people realise the importance of. Man has enjoyed the beauty and benefits of plants for centuries. In our quest for a better and healthier environment today, we are beginning to feel the impact and value trees and other plants much more for their contributions are beyond mere beauty.

Trees, in much broader terms, may be said to give character to cities, streets and buildings, particularly the environment we live in.

Trees and shrubs, to most people, are often taken to mean only chunks of greenery, merely to fill up a void, act as barriers or to give protection or privacy.

Some thoughts should be given to the types of trees, their suitability, their general characteristics, ultimate size and so on. Proper planting distances should be observed and due regard must be given to space availability. All these are pertinent points to consider before any planting exercise is undertaken. The problem is that planters do not pay enough attention to the future. Too often owners crave for immediate effects at the expense of proper and healthy plant growth and development.

This book has been conceived with the purpose of providing quick reference for plant lovers and other interested parties of the wide variety of beautiful plant materials that are available for landscape usage in the Malaysian context. It will stimulate an awareness amongst property developers and garden enthusiasts of the vital role landscape planting can play in the years to come. For what is planted today shall be the legacy to be shared and enjoyed by future generations.

Lam Peng Sam

Acknowledgement

This book would not have been possible without the kind and generous assistance of my friends. I wish to thank Johan Smith and Lam Peng Sam, a retired horticulturist, for reading and editing the manuscript. And to my wife and sons, I dedicate this book.

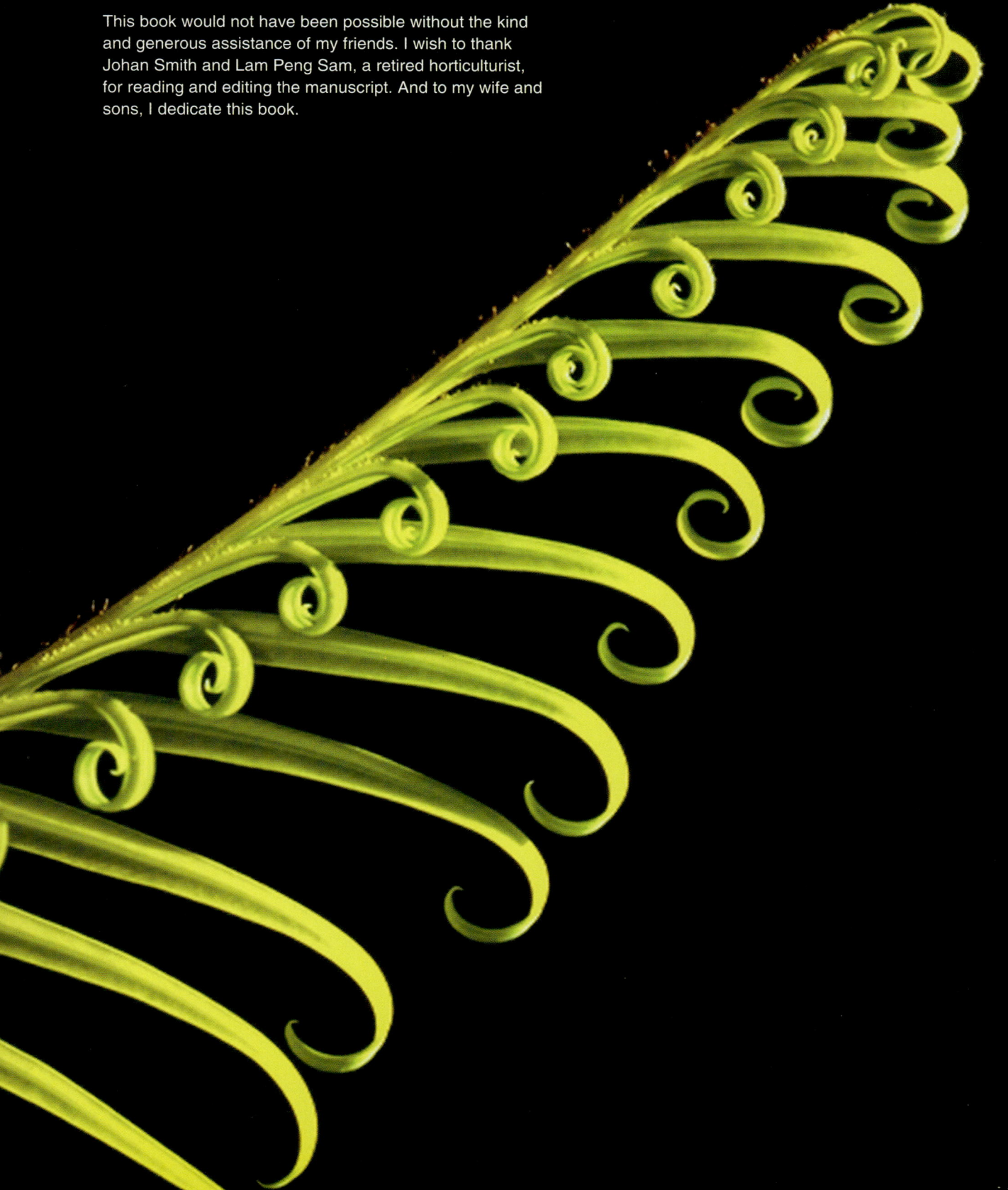

Preface

The aim of this book was conceived as a guide to those who are interested to plant trees and shrubs. For those who are planning for housing estates, park lands and even the compound of condominiums and offices or shopping complexes, there are no reference books which are easily available in the market. This book will be useful to assist one to choose the kind of trees or shrubs for the kind of gardens which are being designed for some specific areas. Buildings without trees or shrubs among them would be like an unfinished picture without its frame. Someone said "Whenever we plant a tree, we are doing what we can to make the place we live in a more wholesome and happier environment for those who come after us if not for ourselves".

The English poet, Tennyson described the life history of a tree as follows:

Ho! in the middle of the wood,
the folded leaf is wood from
out the bud
with winds upon the branch
and there grows green and broad,
and takes no care
sun-steep at noon,
and in the moon nightly dew-fed;
and turning yellow falls
and floats adown the air.

In our fast growing society, one must make time to admire a tree.

Such as, the lovely matured palm or a tall slender tree that grows in a rugged grandeur on the edge of the escarpment is a majestic object to behold, especially against a setting sun.

Trees and plants add interest and life to a building and enhance its aesthetic value, which would otherwise, be lifeless and uninteresting. They give colour and shade contrast to the often hard surface of stone, concrete, brick or metal surfaces of a building.

These trees and plants around a building bring out the character and feature at its best. They add beauty and quality of life to the surroundings and create an atmosphere of serenity which is a most coveted commodity in our present day living. However, in order to preserve the beauty of trees and plants, constant maintenance and proper care become necessary. Without the right kind of maintenance trees and plants that form the beautiful landscape will be short-lived.

In conclusion, the right choice of trees and plants and proper maintenance will ensure the lasting beauty of a landscape so that it will always be there for all to enjoy. It is important to select the right kind of tree for the right location and one should never overlook the significance of providing constant and proper maintenance.

The Author

Ong Guan Teck was born in Sarawak, Malaysia. He obtained his education at St Thomas School, Kuching and University of Melbourne, Victoria, Australia.

He is a member of the British Institute of Architects, Fellowship of the Royal Australian Institute of Architects and as well as a corporate member of the Pertubuhan Akitek Malaysia.

He has worked extensively as an architect in Australia and Malaysia. He won the First Aga Khan World Award for Islamic Architecture on Tanjong Jara Beach Hotel Complex, Dungun, Terengganu in 1983.

Contents

Foreword
Acknowledgement
Preface
The Author

TREES

Acacia auriculiformis	Wattle, Yellow Acacia 1
Acacia mangium	Broadleaf Acacia 2
Alstonia angustiloba	Pokok Pulai 3
Araucaria excelsa	Norfolk Pine 4
Bauhinia blakeana	Butterfly Tree 5
Casuarina nobile	Pokok Ru Roneng 6
Cerbera odollam	Pong-Pong Tree 7
Cinnamomum iners	Wild Cinnamon, Medang Teja, Pokok Manis 8
Cyathea spp	Lowland Tree Fern 9
Delonix regia	Semarak Api, Flame of the Forest 10
Erythrina glauca	Pokok Dedap 11
Erythrina variegata	Variegated Coral Tree, Pokok Dedap, Dedap Batik 12
Ficus maclellandi	Long Leaf Ficus 13
Ficus varigata	Golden Leaves 14
Filicium decipiens	Fern-leaved Tree 15
Fragraea fragrans	Pokok Tembusu 16
Michelia alba	Chempaka Putih 17
Mimusops elengi	Bunga Tanjung 18
Peltophorum pterocarpum	Yellow Flame, Batai Laut, Jemerlang 19
Persea americana	Avocado Pear Tree 20
Pithecellobium dulce	Madras Thorn 21
Plumeria acuminata	Frangipani 22
Polyalthia longifolia	Mast Tree 23
Pterocarpus indicus	Angsana, Sena 24
Ravenala magascariensis	Traveller's Palm 25
Sterculia foetida	Pokok Kelumpang 26
Syzgium malaccense	Jambu Bol 27

SHRUBS

Acalypha siamensis	Siamese Acalypha, Tea Leaves 29
Acalypha wilkinsiana	Acalypha (Red Leaf Type) or Hawaiian Acalypha 30
Acalypha wilkinsiana	Acalypha (Yellow Green Variegated Type) 31
Allamanda cathartica	Yellow Bells 32
Averrhoa bilimbi	Bilimbing Asam 33
Bambusa nana	Hedge Bamboo, Bamboo Pagar 34
Bougainvillea	Bunga Kertas, Mary Palmer Bougainvillea 35
Bougainvillea glabra variegata	Variegated Bougainvillea 36
Bougainvillea spectabilis	Golden Bougainvillea, Variegated Bougainvillea 37
Caesalpinia pulcherrima	Peacock Flower, Pride of Barbados 38
Callistemon lanceolatus	Bottle Brush 39
Cassia spectabilis	Scented Cassia 40
Cassia surattensis	Glaucous Cassia 41
Codiaeum puntatum aureum	Golden dwarf codiaeum 42
Cordyline terminalis	Red Edge 43
Cythula prostrata	Cythula Groundcover 44
Dracaena marginata	Rainbow Fern 45
Ficus benjamina variegata	Variegated Ficus 46
Ficus nitida variegata	Golden-Leaved Ficus 47
Hibiscus rosa sinensis	Hibiscus, Bunga Raya 48

Hibiscus rosa sinensis (Cooperi)	Cotton Leaf Hibiscus 49
Hibiscus rosa sinensis (crested)	Chicken Crest Hibiscus 50
Ixora "sunkiss"	Small Siantan 51
Ixora chinensis	Ixora 52
Ixora coccinea (yellow)	Yellow Ixora 53
Lagerstroemia indica	Inai Merah, Crepe Myrtle 54
Lantana montevidensis	Bunga Misi 55
Lochnera rosea (Vinca rosea, Catharanthus rosea)	Periwinkle, Kemunting Cina 56
Pandanus pygmaeus	Golden Pygmy 57
Phyllanthus myrtifolius	Phyllanthus, Mouse Tail Plant 58
Pisonia alba	Mengkudu Siani, Lettuce Tree 59
Plumbago capensis	Plumbago Blue 60
Polyscias filicifolia	Golden Polyscias 61
Pseudoeranthemum reticulatum	Golden Leaves Flower 62
Rhoeo spathacea	Purple Leaf Herb 63

PALMS

Archontophoenix alexandrae	King Palm, Alexandra Palm 65
Areca catechu	Pokok Pinang, Betel Nut Palm 66
Borasus flabellifer	Lontar, Palmyra Palm or Sea Coconut 67
Chrysalidocarpus lutescens	Yellow Cane Palm, Madagascar Palm 68
Cocos nucifera	Coconut, Kelapa 69
Cycas revoluta	Cycad Palm 70
Cyrtostachys lakka	Pinang Rajah, Candle Wax Palm 71
Lantania loddigesii	Madagascar Palm 72
Latania lontaroides	Golden Net Palm 73
Livistona chinensis	Pokok Serdang, Chinese Fan Palm 74
Livistona rotundifolia	Serdang, Malayan Fan Palm 75
Mascarena lagenicaulis	Champagne Bottle Palm 76
Ptychosperma macarthurii	Macarthur Palm 77
Rhapis excelsa	Lady Palm 78
Roystonea oleracca	Cabbage Palm 79
Roystonea regia	Royal Palm 80
Tables	81
Index	84
Reference	85

Botanical Name *Acacia auriculiformis*
Local Name Wattle, Yellow Acacia

Characteristics

It is an evergreen tree and fast growing. It is sometimes mistaken for *Acacia cicinnata* as it is very similar when young. Its light brown bark is fairly clear. Its small yellow flowers are very insignificant similar to that of *Acacia cicinnata* flowers. Propagation is by seed.

Height of Growth

It can grow up to 45 metres high.

Recommended Planting Position

It is not recommended for small gardens unless it is constantly trimmed. It is suitable for park lands and wide road shoulders. Wood is not strong enough to withstand high winds — liable to break.

Botanical Name *Acacia mangium*
Local Name Broadleaf Acacia

Characteristics

This is a fast growing evergreen tree and can grow up to 20 metres high. It originated from Papua New Guinea and Queensland, Australia. It was brought over from Sabah and sometimes it is called Sabah Acacia. Its broad leaves are 3cm × 15cm long and dark green in colour with distinctive white veins. Its fluffy white flowers produced in clusters are spike-like in the axils of the phyllodes. It flowers generally in the months of October and November.

Recommended Planting Position

As its trunk is clean and strong with a good crown, it can be planted for good shade in a large garden. It can also be planted as a wind-break along the fence.

Botanical Name *Alstonia angustiloba*
Local Name Pokok Pulai

Characteristics

This is a fast growing tree and originated from Sumatra, Indonesia and Malaysia. Its straight trunk is light brown and clean. It is a deciduous tree and sheds its leaves once a year. Its sap can be used for gum on trapping of small birds. When its main top trunk is pruned, its branches spread out as an umbrella. It has strong tap root.

Height of Growth

It grows up to 60 metres if it is left unmaintained and unpruned.

Recommended Planting Position

It is suitable for large gardens and park lands especially on the western aspect. Its roots can cause damage to any pavement and it can be adapted to any soil condition.

Botanical Name *Araucaria excelsa*
Local Name Norfolk Pine

Characteristics
   This tree has its branches spread out horizontally at low level of its trunk. It is easy to identify this pine tree. The leaves are long (2cm) and curved inwards towards the stem.

Height of Growth
   This tree can grow up to 40 metres without any interruption.

Recommended Planting Position
   This tree can be planted in open park lands and large gardens where light shade is needed.

Botanical Name *Bauhinia blakeana*
Local Name Butterfly Tree

Characteristics
It is a fast growing tree with fairly large leaves about 7.5cm. It has pale purple to pink coloured flowers. It provides light shade because the branches and leaves are not dense.

Height of Growth
It can grow from 7 metres to 10 metres high.

Recommended Planting Position
It is suitable to plant in the front garden provided it is maintained regularly by pruning overgrown branches. It is best grown on the eastern aspect of the garden where it is not exposed to hot afternoon sun.

TROPICAL TREES AND SHRUBS PLANTING

Botanical Name *Casuarina nobile*
Local Name Pokok Ru Roneng

Characteristics
This is the best looking pine tree with its fine needle-like leaves which form a good foliage of dark green colour. It has a symmetrical bushy crown. Sometimes it can be trimmed to shape. It grows well on sandy soil or well-drained soil in sunny position. It forms a good screen hedge and provides shade when planted closely together. Its origin is from Sarawak.

Height of Growth
It can grow up to 15 metres or more depending on its environment.

Recommended Planting Position
It is suitable for planting in house gardens, parks and roadside tables on the western aspect.

Botanical Name *Cerbera odollam*
Local Name Pong-Pong Tree

Characteristics

This is a fast growing tree and grows well on sandy soil where it is a bit damp. Its leaves are fairly large 20cm long and 10cm wide, and rounded at the edge. The green leaves are glossy. It has fruits like the size of an apple and are red when they are ripe. They are poisonous. Its flowers are white. The tree has a short trunk.

Height of Growth

It grows usually up to 12 metres high.

Recommended Planting Position

It can grow in full sun and is suitable for car parks although its leaves fall during the dry weather. The round crown of the tree gives fairly good shade. It is not recommended for small gardens.

TROPICAL TREES AND SHRUBS PLANTING

Botanical Name *Cinnamomum iners*
Local Name Wild Cinnamon, Medang Teja, Pokok Manis

Characteristics
    It is a medium growing tree with dense foliage. Its attractiveness comes from its young leaves which are pink in colour before they turn into dark green. However, its flowers are very small and creamy in colour. The trunk is clear and needs to have some pruning to keep the tree in good shape. Native to Peninsular Malaysia.

Height of Growth
    It can grow up to 15 metres high.

Recommended Planting Position
    It forms a good screen for a large garden when planted about 3 metres apart. It gives good shade. One of the best for home gardens.

Botanical Name *Cyathea spp*
Local Name Lowland Tree Fern

Characteristics

This fern grows like a tree with its long and slender trunk. The leaves grow on the end of the trunk resembling branches of a tree. The trunk is usually covered with interwoven roots and these form the tough fibrous trunk. Propagation is by wind-borne spores which are enclosed in minute capsules called sporangia.

Height of Growth

It usually grows up to 4 metres high under semi-shade.

Recommended Planting Position

It can be quite decorative if planted by the side of an artificial fountain or a running stream with some rock boulders.

Botanical Name *Delonix regia*
Local Name Semarak Api, Flame of the Forest

Characteristics

This tree is slow growing from seed. The tree is deciduous and the large red flowers are produced when new leaves emerge near the end of its branches. It flowers well in dry weather conditions. It can grow to 18 metres high in open space and in full sun.

Recommended Planting Position

It is suitable to plant in large gardens as a feature when it is blooming. The tree needs strong sunlight to develop properly.

Botanical Name *Erythrina glauca*
Local Name Pokok Dedap

Characteristics

It is a quick growing tree with short woody spines on its trunk. As a deciduous tree, its leaves fall during dry season once or more each year. It has dark green leaves and produces fairly good shape when fully grown. It has scarlet red flowers in contrast to its leaves. It can be propagated by cuttings.

Height of Growth

It can grow up to 15 metres high.

Recommended Planting Position

It is a fairly clean tree and can be planted in the western aspect of a garden.

Botanical Name *Erythrina variegata*
Local Name Variegated Coral Tree, Pokok Dedap, Dedap Batik

Characteristics

This is a fast growing tree. It has large leaves with yellow stripes which make it attractive. The trunk has small spiny twigs which can be hurtful to children. The foliage forms a good shady umbrella over a large area. It is a hardy tree and can withstand any soil condition.

Height of Growth

It can grow up to 15 metres or more when it is fully matured.

Recommended Planting Position

It is not recommended for small gardens. However, it is suitable to plant in open car parks and roadside.

Botanical Name *Ficus maclellandi*
Local Name Long Leaf Ficus

Characteristics

This is a fast growing tree. Its leaves are dark green with a white stripe in the centre. Its fruits are small and round and turn yellow when ripe. This tree can grow up to 10 metres high if not encumbered by other trees.

Recommended Planting Position

It gives good shade for a large garden. Drooping branches need to be trimmed to keep in shape. It is a clean tree and is seldom subject to insect attack. However, because of its spreading roots, they should not be planted less than 5 metres from the house or any property.

Botanical Name *Ficus varigata*
Local Name Golden Leaves

Characteristics
   This tree has yellow young leaves. Leaflets are bent downwards and gradually become green to dark green as the leaves get older.

Height of Growth
   If not pruned, it can grow up to 5 metres high. However, it looks its best at a height of not more than 1.5 metres.

Recommended Planting Position
   This shrub can be planted to complement any long trunk trees or palms in a garden or pool deck area.

Botanical Name *Filicium decipiens*
Local Name Fern leaved tree

Characteristics
    This is a fast growing tree with dark green foliage spreading out. It has a clean short trunk and often has branches which need to be trimmed back. Leaves are feather-like.

Height of Growth
    It can grow up to 20 metres high if left alone without pruning.

Recommended Planting Position
    Large house gardens, roadside and park lands. It gives good shade. It can adapt itself in most type of soil conditions.

TROPICAL TREES AND SHRUBS PLANTING

Botanical Name *Fragraea fragrans*
Local Name Pokok Tembusu

Characteristics

A slow growing tree with light green leaves usually 13cm to 5cm wide. It has small cream-coloured fragrant flowers. It is an evergreen. Propagation is by seed.

Height of Growth

It can grow up to 30 metres high and gives semi-shade.

Recommended Planting Position

It can be planted singly or in a row to form high hedges or wind-break. It is not suitable for small gardens.

Botanical Name *Michelia alba*
Local Name Chempaka Putih

Characteristics
This is a fast growing tree originated from Java, Indonesia. Sometimes its flowers are yellow-orange in colour and it is called *chempakah merah*. Leaves are usually 25cm long × 15cm wide and flowers are 5.0cm wide with narrow petals on short stalks and are fragrant especially at night. It is an evergreen tree.

Height of Growth
It can grow up to 21 metres high without much maintenance.

Recommended Planting Position
It is not recommended for small gardens, but it gives good shade. It is best planted by the roadside or in parks. Propagation is by cuttings, marcotting and budding.

TROPICAL TREES AND SHRUBS PLANTING

Botanical Name   *Mimusops elengi*
Local Name   Bunga Tanjung

Characteristics

This is a fast growing tree, originated from India, Ceylon and Burma and is an evergreen. Its large leaves are 15cm long × 7.5cm wide. Its small white flowers are fragrant but insignificant as its foliage is usually very dense. Its trunk grows straight and its spreading branches need to be pruned to keep in good shape. It is propagated by seed.

Height of Growth

This tree can grow up to 20 metres high.

Recommended Planting Position

This tree gives good shade and can be planted in open car parks, large gardens where shade is needed. It thrives well on sandy soil and requires little maintenance.

Botanical Name   *Peltophorum pterocarpum*
Local Name   Yellow Flame, Batai Laut, Jemerlang

Characteristics

It is a medium growing tree with small leaves to form a dense foliage. It has brillant yellow flowers. If it is well watered and maintained it provides good shade. It changes its leaves once a year during the dry season. Native to Peninsular Malaysia.

Height of Growth

It can grow up to 45 metres.

Recommended Planting Position

It is suitable for medium to large gardens but not good for small gardens because of its dropping of leaves and flowers. However, large open spaces and parks will be more appropriate for planting.

TROPICAL TREES AND SHRUBS PLANTING

Botanical Name   *Persea americana*
Local Name   Avocado Pear Tree

Characteristics

The tree grows reasonably fast. It can be budded for planting. The leaves are dark green and its fruits are pear-shaped, 7 to 20cm long and yellowish green in colour. Propagation is by budding or by seeds. Flowers are usually 1.3cm, fragrant and yellow in colour. Native to Tropical America.

Height of Growth

It can grow up to 20 metres if it is not pruned. It forms a good shade.

Recommended Planting Position

It is recommended to plant it in the western aspect of the garden or by the side of an entrance to the building.

Botanical Name *Pithecellobium dulce*
Local Name Madras Thorn

Characteristics

This is a fast growing tree. Its leaves are fairly small, light green to dark green in colour. The trunk is short and has many branches. As the leaves are small, the fallen ones generally rot away and require minimum maintenance. It has a large crown and thus provides fairly good shade. It originated from tropical America. Branches are thorny.

Height of Growth

It can grow to 15 metres high without any hindrance.

Recommended Planting Position

It is suitable to plant in open car parks or large gardens. It is also attractive to plant on the road shoulder.

Botanical Name *Plumeria acuminata*
Local Name Frangipani

Characteristics
This is a stout tree with strong trunk. The tree has a compacted crown and provides reasonable shade. There are three main species namely *Plumeria obtusa* (white flower with yellow centre), *Plumeria Acuta* (pink flower with yellow centre) and *Plumeria rubra* (dark pink to red with yellow centre). The *Plumeria obtusa* bears the most flowers.

Height of Growth
The tree can grow from 5 metres to 6 metres high.

Recommended Planting Position
This tree can withstand very dry soil condition and can be planted in large gardens and parks or road shoulders as a flowering tree.

Botanical Name *Polyalthia longifolia*
Local Name Mast Tree

Characteristics
    This is a reasonably fast growing tree with drooping leaves hanging from the sides of its trunk. When fully matured, its appearance is conical in shape as it has a pointed crown. The leaves are long, 15cm × 5cm wide with serrated edges on both sides and dark green in colour. It does not give good shade.

Height of Growth
    It can grow up to 15 metres high or more if the tree is not interrupted by pruning.

Recommended Planting Position
    It is suitable for high hedges, planting in rows or clusters along the boundaries of a garden or park. It can be grown together with other smaller shrubs.

Botanical Name *Pterocarpus indicus*
Local Name Angsana, Sena

Characteristic

This is a common fast growing tree. It is native to Peninsular Malaysia. Its leaves are fairly large, 15cm long × 10cm wide. It has a large crown and forms good shade in full sun. However, it has to be well-maintained by pruning its branches and not to let it grow more than 20 metres high. Otherwise, it becomes straggly. It can be propagated by cuttings.

Height of Growth

It can grow up to 30 metres or higher if the lower branches are cut periodically.

Recommended Planting Position

It is suitable to plant in open car parks and large road shoulders. They must be properly maintained but are not suitable for small gardens.

Botanical Name *Ravenala magascariensis*
Local Name Traveller's Palm

Characteristics

This plant is not a true palm. It belongs to the Musasae family to which bananas and heliconias belong. This plant has its leaves spread out like a peacock's tail or a fan; thus is known as a traveller's fan "palm". The leaves, at the end of the long stalks are known as petioles and have the appearance of banana leaves. It does not flower in Malaysia and propagation is by its young sucker shoots coming out from the base of the "palm". It is a fast growing plant and can withstand adverse weather conditions.

Height of Growth

It can grow up to 20 metres high but will lose its majestic appearance if it grows too high.

Recommended Planting Position

It is suitable to plant it as a feature plant in house gardens or park lands. They can be planted in clusters or in rows to form an avenue along a foot path. It grows well in a sheltered position.

Botanical Name *Sterculia foetida*
Local Name Pokok Kelumpang

Characteristics

This is a fast growing tree with fairly large green leaves, about 15cm long × 7.5cm wide, on long stalks. It has a straight and long trunk which is dark brown in colour. Its flowers are insignificant but its fruits, about 2.5cm, are round and dark red when they are ripe. Its seeds are black in colour. It is a deciduous tree.

Height of Growth

It can grow up to 35 metres high with an oval crown.

Recommended Planting Position

It is not recommended for small gardens despite its attractive red fruits. It can be planted along the roadside and in park lands and gives reasonable shade.

Botanical Name *Syzgium malaccense*
Local Name Jambu Bol

Characteristics

This is a fast growing tree with large green leaves about 7 to 17cm wide × 1.5cm long. Its trunk is light brown with clean bark. Its red flowers are attractive to birds and insects. It forms a very dense foliage when it is fully matured and columnar in habit.

Height of Growth

It can grow up to 20 metres high when planted in an open garden.

Recommended Planting Position

As it forms a good shade, it can be planted in the western aspect of the garden. It can withstand dry condition. It is not recommended for a small garden.

SHRUBS

Shrubs may be arbitrarily classified under small trees. There is really no sharp distinction between trees and shrubs. Generally anything less than 2 metres high are considered shrubs, after which they are categorised as tree-shrubs and on to small trees which are usually up to 3-4 metres high. Basically, shrubs are less erect in habit, much more bushy in character, and have greater rigour and luxuriance in growth. Shrubs are usually planted to complement tall and slender trunk trees. The best shrubs are evergreen because they form a background setting for trees or flowers planted amongst them.

It is also possible to trim shrubs to bush-form (multi-stemmed) to adopt a tree-form (single-stemmed or trunk) for many years to serve a particular function.

There are always shrubs to fit every situation, especially for small gardens where even one small tree is impossible and this is where a tall shrub transformed to a single-stemmed "tree" can play an important role.

Botanical Name   *Acalypha siamensis*
Local Name   Siamese Acalypha, Tea Leaves

Characteristics

This is a fast growing plant. Its small greenish leaves are serated on both sides. It can be propagated by cuttings and grows well on sandy or well-drained soil in full sun. It can grow up to 1.2 metres high.

Recommended Planting Position

It forms a good hedge when they are planted at 30cm apart. The plants can be trimmed to shape for an open garden.

Botanical Name *Acalypha wilkinsiana*
Local Name Acalypha (Red Leaf Type) or Hawaiian Acalypha

Characteristics
   This is a fast growing plant and can grow up to 2 to 3 metres high in open space. It has small and insignificant flowers but its leaves are multicoloured with yellow, red and green. Other species include the red-leaf and green-leaf varieties.

Recommended Planting Position
   It can be planted closely as a hedge or in the centre of a garden as a feature. It looks well against any white wall of a building.

Botanical Name *Acalypha wilkinsiana*
Local Name   Acalypha (Yellow green Variegated type)

Characteristics

This is a fast growing plant and can grow up to 2 to 3 metres high in open space. It has small and insignificant flowers but its leaves are green and contrasting yellow. Other species include the red-leaf and green-leaf varieties.

Recommended Planting Position

It can be planted closely as a hedge or in the centre of a garden as a feature. It looks well against any white wall of a building.

TROPICAL TREES AND SHRUBS PLANTING

Botanical Name *Allamanda cathartica*
Local Name Yellow Bells

Characteristics

This shrub has 3 or 4 leaflets growing out from a point. Its golden yellow flowers often grow between the leaves. It can withstand hot sun. It is a perennial. Another species is *Allamanda schottii* with a more erect habit and grows about 60cm tall. These plants can complement a backdrop of green or dark red-coloured plants.

Height of Growth

It can grow up to 1.5 metres if it is not pruned and grown in an open space.

Recommended Planting Position

It can be planted as a feature shrub in the garden, large pots or in rows to present a good continuous yellow colour against any back drop of building or plants.

Botanical Name   *Averrhoa bilimbi*
Local Name   Bilimbing Asam

Characteristics

This small tree has clear, pinkish bark on a short trunk which breaks into branches at a height of about 1.2 metres high. Fruits are about 5cm long. The leaves are light green divided into leaflets and bunched together at the end of the twigs. Flowers are about 2.5cm long × 2.5 wide and pinkish white in colour. The crown of the tree is often rounded and is a native to Malaysia. Fruits are edible.

Height of Growth

It can grow up to 6 metres high and give a good shade.

Recommended Planting Position

It grows well in well-drained soil in sunny position of the house garden.

Botanical Name   *Bambusa nana*
Local Name   Hedge Bamboo, Bamboo Pagar

Characteristics
    This is a fast growing plant and if it is not pruned it can grow up to 3 to 4 metres high. Its leaves are small, usually 7.5cm long × 1.2cm wide and light green in colour. It is evergreen though its leaves drop fairly regularly.

Height of Growth
    It can grow up to 4 metres if it is not interrupted by pruning.

Recommended Planting Position
    It is suitable for hedges along the boundaries of a building. However, it has to be constantly trimmed. It can also be planted as a feature plant in a large garden.

Botanical Name *Bougainvillea*
Local Name Bunga Kertas, Mary Palmer Bougainvillea

Characteristics

This scrambling shrub can grow up to 15 metres if planted in the open. It has many hybrids such as *Bougainvillea buttiana* (Gold Yellow), *Bougainvillea buttiana* "Mrs Butt" – dark red flowers and variegated leaves, *Bougainvillea spectabilis* (Lateritia Gold), etc.

Recommended Planting Position

It is not recommended to be planted in concrete planters which are not exposed to full sun. Constant pruning and manuring is required for the plant to bloom properly. It is best to be planted in full sun and open gardens.

Botanical Name   *Bougainvillea glabra variegata*
Local Name   Variegated Bougainvillea

Characteristics

This plant is a quick growing shrub but it does not flower well. Its leaves have light yellow edges and light green centres.

Recommended Planting Position

This plant is best planted in a planter box with other dark green/white leaves. Although, it does not flower well, its leaves form an attractive feature for the garden.

SHRUBS

Botanical Name *Bougainvillea spectabilis*
Local Name Golden Bougainvillea, Variegated Bougainvillea

Characteristics
This is an attractive plant with white edged leaves and can become a creeper if left to grow on its own (unpruned). Its light purple flowers are usually borne at the ends of its branches.

Recommended Planting Position
It is recommended to plant in front of a house entrance in full sun. If it is constantly pruned, the plant will bloom better. It grows well in sandy soil and should be well-watered.

Botanical Name   *Caesalpinia pulcherrima*
Local Name   Peacock Flower, Pride of Barbados

Characteristics
This is a flowering shrub with light green divided leaves. It can be found in most tropical countries. Its flowers are bright orange in erect terminal inflorescences. Its clawed petals are attractive feature of this plant. It needs to be pruned at least once a year to keep the plant in good shape.

Height of Growth
It grows up to 5 metres high in full sun.

Recommended Planting Position
It is suitable for front gardens and requires minimum maintenance. It can be propagated by seed. It tolerates poor soil conditions. Requires full sun.

Botanical Name *Callistemon lanceolatus*
Local Name Bottle Brush

Characteristics

This is a slow growing tree and has a strong trunk. It has a thick crown when the tree is fully matured. The branches though spread out are drooping. The bright red flowers have the likeness of a bottle brush and fluffy in appearance. The name Callistemon is derived from the Greek words *kallos* - beauty and *stemon* - stamen. It originated from Australia. It is an evergreen tree.

Height of Growth

It can grow up to 8 metres high and has fairly dense foliage.

Recommended Planting Position

This tree prefers well-drained soil and is suitable for the house garden as a feature tree or in the park lands. This tree attracts small birds.

Botanical Name *Cassia spectabilis*
Local Name Scented Cassia

Characteristics
This is a fast growing shrub and grows well in well-drained soil. It can grow up to 6 metres high.

Recommended Planting Position
It can be grown in large gardens in order to give a semi-shade or as an attraction. However, it is not recommended for small gardens because it occupies too large a space.

Botanical Name *Cassia surattensis*
Local Name Glaucous Cassia

Characteristics

This is a fast growing shrub and grows well in well-drained soil. It can grow up to 4 metres high but it does not flower as well as *Cassia biflora*.

Recommended Planting Position

It can be grown in large gardens to give a semi-shade or as an attraction. However, it is not recommended for small gardens because it becomes untidy during fruiting time and can be very straggly.

TROPICAL TREES AND SHRUBS PLANTING

Botanical Name *Codiaeum puntatum aureum*
Local Name Golden dwarf codiaeum

Characteristics

This is a dense and bushy plant, remains dwarfish in size for the first 6-9 months, growing no taller than 30-45cm. Leaves are very narrow and linear. They are dark glossy green or golden yellow and leathery. Some varieties freely spotted polka-dot fashion, while others may be deep maroon with orange combination.

Recommended Planting Position

Suitable for mass planting in beds in full sunshine for vibrant colours. Ideal as potted specimens.

SHRUBS

Botanical Name *Cordyline terminalis*
Local Name Red Edge

Characteristics

This is a plant that grows very well and produces its best reddish to purple leaves. It has about 20 species ranging from dark green leaves to yellow and pink centres type. It can grow straight upwards to 3 metres high. Its trunk is usually slender.

Recommended Planting Position

They can be planted in a cluster in the centre of the garden to create a central garden interest. They are also suitable to be planted in planter boxes but must be in full sun.

Botanical Name *Cythula prostrata*
Local Name Cythula Groundcover

Characteristics

This is a fast growing creeper plant. Its leaves are fairly large and are chocolate-purple in colour. It can grow to 60cm.

Recommended Planting Position

It is a good groundcover with colour to complement any long trunk palm or tree.

SHRUBS

Botanical Name *Dracaena marginata*
Local Name Rainbow Fern

Characteristics

This is a slow growing plant and it can reach up to 5 metres high. Its leaves are long and narrow usually dark green and pink. Another variety has light with faint yellow edges, and yellow central streaks with pink edges (*Dracaena marginata* (Tricolour)).

Recommended Planting Position

It is recommended to be planted in large concrete planter boxes in full sun to bring out the best colour of the plants. It gives good relief to standard rigid planting in the garden. Also an ideal pot plant.

Botanical Name   *Ficus benjamina variegata*
Local Name   Variegated Ficus

Characteristics

This plant has whitish yellow edges on its leaves with central white spine-like veins. It can grow up to 3 metres high in open gardens in full sun. Its trunk is usually light grey.

Recommended Planting Position

It can grow well in large flower pots or planter boxes for small gardens as a feature in the garden.

Botanical Name *Ficus nitida variegata*
Local Name Golden-Leaved Ficus

Characteristics

This is a fast growing shrub and can grow up to 3 metres when left alone in the open sun.

Recommended Planting Position

It makes a good hedge and can decorate a dull fence. It gives out its colour best in full sun. The attractive part is when the plant is carefully trimmed. It forms a compact bushy plant with bright yellow leaves at its crown.

Botanical Name *Hibiscus rosa sinensis*
Local Name Hibiscus, Bunga Raya

Characteristics

This is a fast growing plant and usually grows up to 3 metres high. There are many varieties of hybrid hibiscus. Their flowers range from white to dark red. The flower has 5 petals usually with a central long staminal column with yellow stamens and 5-lobed stigma at the end. Others have multi-petals like a rose flower such as *jermes inoplenus*. A hardy shrub and is rarely attacked by disease.

Recommended Planting Position

They can be planted as a hedge against a fence, or in clusters in the centre of a garden. They also make attractive roadside plants and need constant pruning to flower well.

Botanical Name *Hibiscus rosa sinensis (Cooperi)*
Local Name Cotton Leaf Hibiscus

Characteristics

This is a variegated hibiscus species which seldom bear flowers but grown for its multi-coloured leaves. It can grow up to 2 metres high in full sun.

Recommended Planting Position

It is recommended for low and thick hedges along the boundary fence or in places to demarcate a foot path.

Botanical Name   *Hibiscus rosa sinensis (crested)*
Local Name   Chicken Crest Hibiscus

Characteristics
This is a fast growing plant and will grow up to 2 metres high. Flowers are generally scarce but its attractiveness comes from its variegated leaves. Its flowers are usually pink to white colour.

Recommended Planting Position
It is well-suited to good drainage soil and in full sun. The plant can be used as a special feature in the centre of a garden. It grows better with constant trimming and manuring after flowering.

Botanical Name *Ixora "sunkiss"*
Local Name Small Siantan

Characteristics
The flower is characterised by a long slender corolla tube which opens into four lanceolate petals. This species has small and pointed petals radiating from the centre. Very free flowering.

Recommended Planting Position
It is best to plant in clusters in full sun in front of the house. It likes sandy and well-drained soil.

Botanical Name *Ixora chinensis*
Local Name Ixora

Characteristics
This is a broad-leaved plant with its flowers forming a large bouquet of about 15cm diameter. It can grow up to 1.2 metres high and it blooms well after pruning and application of fertiliser.

Recommended Planting Position
It blooms well in full sun, in sandy and well-drained soil. It is suitable near the seaside, in hotel resorts or condominium compound.

Botanical Name *Ixora coccinea (yellow)*
Local Name Yellow Ixora

Characteristics

This plant has broad leaves similar to the Red Ixora. However, it flowers as well as the red species. It grows well in sandy or well-drained soil. It is suitable to grow in plant-boxes. Requires good well-drained soil and high moisture level for healthy growth.

Recommended Planting Position

It is an attractive plant and is suitable to grow in front of a house garden especially against a white wall. It flowers well in full sun.

Botanical Name *Lagerstroemia indica*
Local Name Inai Merah, Crepe Myrtle

Characteristics

This is a fast growing shrub which grows on a long stem in rows. The leaves are small and dark green in colour. Its flowers bloom at the end of the long stems in bunches of pink. It likes open space and full sun.

Height of Growth

It can grow up to 1.2 metres high when it is time for the plant to bloom.

Recommended Planting Position

It is usually planted along the central divider of a double carriage way road. It is suitable for house gardens and it blooms well but requires regular pruning to bring out better flowering capacity.

Botanical Name *Lantana montevidensis*
Local Name Bunga Misi

Characteristics

This plant is a creeper with thorny stems and branches. Hybrid Lantana has white, orange and purple flowers, etc. They like well-drained soil and plenty of sun.

Recommended Planting Position

They can be planted in large planter boxes but it has to be well watered. They show their best colours against a white wall background in full sun.

Botanical Name　*Lochnera rosea (Vinca rosea, Catharanthus rosea)*
Local Name　Periwinkle, Kemunting Cina

Characteristics

This is a shrub with single branched stems. The pink flowers bloom at the top of leaf axils. The leaves are dark green and glossy. Each flower is composed of a slender tubular base which opens into five corolla lobes. The white species called *Lochnera rosea* var *alba* can be planted beside it to give contrast. It is a perennial plant and grows well on sandy or well-drained soil. It is a native of most coastal areas of Malaysia and semi-tropical countries.

Height of Growth

It can grow up to 1 metres high if it is well-fertilised.

Recommended Planting Position

It can be grown as a border plant in full sun. As the flowers have single petals, they show well if grown in a cluster.

Botanical Name *Pandanus pygmaeus*
Local Name Golden Pygmy

Characteristics

There are about 600 species of Pandanus and this is a very attractive plant. It grows well in the open and spreads as a groundcover fast. Its long and slender leaves are yellow with a centre green stripe.

Recommended Planting Position

It is suitable to plant as an edging strip to define the boundary of the garden plot. It can be planted in planter boxes but it needs constant watering and full exposure. It grows well in full sun but can be grown in semi-shade as well.

Botanical Name *Phyllanthus myrtifolius*
Local Name Phyllanthus, Mouse Tail Plant

Characteristics

This is a small sprawling woody shrub and has leaflets on a stalk. Its dark green leaves are partially closed or folded at night. To grow well, it needs full sunshine and regular application of fertilisers.

Recommended Planting Position

It is suitable for planting in concrete planters surrounding a building or at balcony level. It makes a good border plant.

Botanical Name *Pisonia alba*
Local Name Mengkudu Siani, Lettuce Tree

Characteristics

This shrub is attractive with greenish-yellow broad leaves about 20cm long and 12cm wide coming to a point. It can be found near the seaside like Trengganu, Kelantan and Kedah. It can withstand full sun.

Height of Growth

It grows up to 8 metres and has a large crown, thus giving good shade.

Recommended Planting Position

It is used as a feature in large gardens together with other plants. It can form a large border in large parks, or highways.

Botanical Name *Plumbago capensis*
Local Name Plumbago Blue

Characteristics
This is a perennial plant with pale blue flowers which blooms throughout the year. Propagation is by semi-woody cuttings. It blooms well after constant pruning. It originated from South Africa. They grow up to 20cm high.

Recommended Planting Position
It can be planted in planter boxes or as a border plant in flower beds. It can withstand full sun but grows best in a sheltered position and also thrives well in wet soil conditions.

Botanical Name *Polyscias filicifolia*
Local Name Golden Polyscias

Characteristics

Its leaves are light green, fairly narrow and long and grows out from its central stem. It has serrated edges on both sides of its leaf. There are many other species which have more rounded leaves, such as *Polyscias balfouriana* (Marginata) and *Polyscias quilfoylee* (Quinquefolia), etc.

Height of Growth

It usually grows up to 1.2 metres high.

Recommended Planting Position

It is suitable to grow in close rows as hedges or to put it with other taller plants as a combination of coloured plants in full sun.

Botanical Name *Pseudoeranthemum reticulatum*
Local Name Golden Leaves Flower

Characteristics

This is an attractive shrub. Its young leaves are bright yellow in colour and as the plant gets older, they turn to green colour with yellow veins. It grows approximately 40-50cm tall. Its small flowers are white with pink centres.

Recommended Planting Position

It grows well on sandy soil in full sun. It can be planted as a border plant in close spacing and shows up best with dark green-leaved plants.

Salvia

but the willowlike leaves lend a fine, feathery texture, then turn a beautiful gold in autumn.

Veronica "Sunny Border Blue"—This crinkle-leaf beauty produces its violet-blue flowers from early summer to early fall.

Irises and daylilies—Choose varieties that rebloom.

Pincushion flower *(Scabiosa columbaria)*—This favorite of butterflies and bees blooms for long periods and offers fine-textured foliage.

Visualize how your choices will look in all seasons and arrange them according to height and season of bloom. Put the tallest ones in the center of a freestanding bed or at the back of the border. Avoid having a huge array of different plants with only one or two of each species. In order to have enough of each plant to make a statement, work in groups of three, five, or seven. Then repeat at least part of that grouping elsewhere in the bed to lend a sense of unity to the overall design.

To give the large perennial garden more structure and to help hold the design together all year long, consider including small shrubs. For the first year, until the perennial bed gets fully going on its own, you'll want to include annuals.

Marie Hofer is the gardening editor for HGTV.com.

GETTING STARTED

Do your homework. Research done now pays off in the springs, summers, and falls to come. Make your selections and create the layout on paper, moving plants around until you're satisfied with the look.

Order the seeds (or tubers). Unless you live next door to a well-stocked perennial grower or nursery, you'll have to order by mail to get the varieties you want—and going the seed route is far cheaper.

Prepare the bed as weather allows. Make sure the soil is well worked, free of weeds, and enriched with organic matter. Don't work when it's wet, however, because that will severely compact and destroy the soil structure.

Prepare to plant. Fall-blooming perennials can bloom their first year if they get an early start; spring- and summer-blooming perennials will bloom their second year. Check the packet label for ideal planting times. When the time is right, start some seeds indoors. Or plant them in a flat, water well, and leave outside. (Make sure you keep the seedbed clear of foot traffic, animals, and birds.) Don't worry about more cold weather to come; most perennials require a period of chill in order to germinate. And if an early thaw triggers germination, protect the young seedlings from further freezes by covering with a cold frame or bringing them indoors.—*M.H.*

3 FOR THE ROAD

SALT LAKE CITY, PHOENIX, & MI

Whether you head for a desert city like Phoenix to escape the dipping a decidedly chilly climate like Minneapolis/St. Paul or Winter Olymp happenings waiting to welcome you this season.

©SLOC PHOTO BY DAVID QUINNEY

Just because it's winter doesn't mean you have to hibernate, dozing by the fire and dreaming of spring. Instead, scrap the nap and pack your bags. There's a lot going on all around the country, and you won't want to miss a beat!

SALT LAKE CITY

Host to the 2002 Winter Olympic Games (February 8–24), Salt Lake City is polished and primed for visitors this winter. Even if you haven't nabbed tickets to the games themselves or to some of the more popular cultural events happening concurrently—such as the Mormon Tabernacle Choir's performance or Itzhak Perlman in concert with the Utah Symphony—you'll find plenty of other options.

Not to mention the fact that if you're in the mood for a little sporting activity of your own, this is one place where on most days you can pound the powder on the ski slopes in the morning and shoot a birdie on the golf course in the afternoon.

- January 10–20 **Sundance Film Festival**, various locations ($7–$10; 801-328-3456, www.sundance.org). This year marks the 20th anniversary of this festival showcasing some of the best new independent films. Prospects for stargazing are equally hot, and if you're lucky, you may even catch a glimpse of local fave Robert Redford.

- January 18–21 **Utah International Auto Expo**, South Towne Exposition Center ($4–$7; 801-484-8845, www.autoshowuse.com). Gear up to see hundreds of 2002 and 2003 model cars, trucks, minivans, and sport utility vehicles, as well as several newly introduced preproduction models, specialty vehicles, and concept cars from more than 26 manufacturers.

NNEAPOLIS/ST. PAUL

*mercury or embrace the cold by choosing
ics host Salt Lake City, you'll find lots of*

BY KATY KOONTZ

Clockwise from left: The majestic Wasatch Mountain Range stand guard above the Salt Lake City skyline; luge and bobsledding will be a popular event at the 2002 Winter Olympics; picturesque Sundance is home to the trend-setting film festival each year.

- January 18–March 17 "**Women Beyond Borders**," Art Access Gallery (free; 888-451-2787, www.saltlake2002.com). Artists from 33 countries started out with identical miniature cedar boxes, then transformed them into these widely divergent works of art that honor women's voices and visions.
- January 21 **The Peking Acrobats Return**, Abravanel Hall ($11–$20; 801-533-6683, www.utahsymphony.org). This world-famous troupe continues a tradition that is more than 2,000 years old, bending, flipping, and twisting their bodies in ways you simply have to see to believe.
- February 1–2 "**Bugs Bunny Bonanza**," Abravanel Hall ($22–$41; 801-533-6683, www.utahsymphony.org). What's up, Doc? The Utah Symphony, that's what! Guest conductor George Daugherty leads the symphony in dozens of Merrie Melodies from the cartoon classics you remember most from your childhood.
- February 1–March 17 "**Discover Navajo: People of the Fourth World**," Rio Grande Depot ($8–$15, or $48 for the family; 888-451-2787, www.saltlake2002.com). Explore the amazingly rich Navajo culture through artists' demonstrations, readings of creation stories, and discussions by a Navajo Code Talker from World War II about how the intricate Navajo language helped the United States win the war.
- February 9–10 **Alvin Ailey American Dance Theater**, Capitol Theatre ($35–$90; 888-451-2787, www.saltlake2002.com). Ever wonder about Flo Jo's mojo? Then sprint to get tickets for this performance, the premiere of a ballet based on the life of Olympic runner Florence Griffith Joyner.
- February 11 **Pete Seeger with Children's Dance Theatre**, Capitol Theatre ($10–$25; 888-451-2787, www.saltlake2002.com). The Rock and

Roll Hall of Famer plays American folk music classics as the members of this troupe of impressive pint-size dancers "Turn, Turn, Turn," not to mention leap, pirouette, and plia.

HAMPTON HOTELS: *A Salt Lake City Directory*
- **Downtown**, 425 South 300 West
- **North**, 2393 South 800 West
- **Murray**, 606 West 4500 South
- **Sandy**, 10690 S. Holiday Park Dr.
- **Layton**, 1702 N. Woodland Park Dr.
- **Tooele**, 461 S. Main

For information and reservations, visit hamptoninn.com or call **1-800-HAMPTON**.

PHOENIX

It's hard not to like a place that offers an average of 300 sunny days a year. Need we say more about Phoenix? Well, we certainly could. For one thing, this city is inundated with golf courses (190 at last count) and resorts (including some of the country's top-rated spas). Nature lovers will enjoy using Phoenix as a base for exploring the surrounding Sonoran Desert via Jeep tours or balloon rides. Art and culture are also attractive draws here and in adjacent sister city Scottsdale, with decidedly strong Native American accents. Arizona is, after all, home to 23 reservations representing 21 different Native American tribes.

- January 12 **Phoenix Coyotes Family Festival**, Phoenix Zoo ($5–$12; 480-473-5600, www.phoenixcoyotes.com). All the players and coaches of the popular Phoenix Coyotes ice hockey team mingle with fans at this event benefiting local charities and nonprofit organizations.

Majestic Arabians are the stars at the Scottsdale Arabian Horse Show.

COURTESY ARABIAN HORSE ASSOCIATION OF ARIZONA

- January 16–20 **Barrett-Jackson Classic Car Auction**, WestWorld of Scottsdale ($10–$20; 480-421-6694, www.barrett-jackson.com). Car enthusiasts from around the world have come here for more than three decades to vie for the chance to slide behind the wheel of some of these classic autos, making this the hottest event of its kind.
- January 21–27 **Phoenix Open 2002 Golf Tournament**, Tournament Players Club of Scottsdale ($20; 602-870-4431, www.phoenixopen.com). This is the golf event of the year in a town where golf rules. The classic PGA Tour event includes a 72-hole tournament, four pro-am events, a skills challenge, pro-celebrity shoot-out, Special Olympics putting contest, and golf clinics for juniors and ladies.
- February 2–3 **Hoop Dance Contest**, Heard Museum ($3–$7; 602-252-8848, www.heard.org). It's the twelfth year for this colorful classic—a Native American dance ritual originally done as part of a healing ceremony that involves intricate maneuvers with as many as several dozen hoops on and around the dancer's body in a single performance. Top Native American dancers from across the continent compete for the title of World Champion Hoop Dancer.
- February 14–17: **Pioria Street Fair and San Gennaro Feast**, Pioria Sports Complex ($5; 623-487-7774, www.royalfestivals.com). The fourth annual street fair in this neighboring community will offer live bands, international food, opportunities for shopping, amusement park rides, a petting zoo, and pony rides.
- February 15–24 **Scottsdale Arabian Horse Show**, WestWorld of Scottsdale ($7–$10; 480-515-1500, www.scottsdaleshow.com). The largest Arabian horse show in the world, this event showcases 2,000 Arabians, half-Arabians, and national show horses.
- March 1–3 **Art Detour 14**, downtown Phoenix (free, including shuttle bus transportation; 602-256-7539, www.artlinkphoenix.com). Some 75 different artists' studios, galleries, and art spaces in Phoenix open their doors to the public for this annual event. Be sure to check out the Mystery Galleries, featuring artists who don't have studios or whose work is not shown in galleries.
- March 13–16 **Carousel Horse Show**, WestWorld of Scottsdale (free; 480-312-6802). This annual show features everything from Tennessee walking horses and Peruvian Pasos to roadsters and even mules.

Visit us at hamptoninn.com

INTERSTATE *EYE*

Cathedral Rock, Sedona, Arizona

Cathedral Rock is just one of the distinctive red rock outcroppings that define the town of Sedona, Arizona—a relaxing two-and-a-half-hour drive from Phoenix (see *3 For the Road* on page 16 for information on current Happenings in Phoenix). Off of Interstate 17 between Phoenix and Flagstaff, take State Route 179 for a scenic 15-mile drive among the cliffs into the heart of Sedona, whose small-town peacefulness belies the many activities available, such as hiking, biking, golfing, gallery hopping, and hot air balloon rides. The Sedona Hampton Inn is centrally located in town on Highway 89A (520) 282-4700.

the much-beloved toy, is a creation of Rhode Island–based Hasbro, Inc., the toy company.) We were greeted at our hotel, the Providence/Warwick-Airport Hampton Inn, by the Mr. Potato Head statue titled *Cloud Nine*.

After checking in at midday, we drove in to Providence Place Mall, a 13-acre mall spanning a highway, a river, and train tracks in the heart of the city. We "forced" our daughters to do a little shopping before heading out into Waterplace Park and Riverwalk. Fans of the television show *Providence* would recognize the Venetian-style footbridges and the gondolas that form the backdrop for scenes in the show.

In the open amphitheater next to the tidal basin we took our seats for a free performance of *The Taming of the Shrew*, an irreverent but highly enjoyable presentation by a youthful company of actors. After the show, as darkness descended, the crowds along the canal grew in anticipation of WaterFire Providence, a magical outdoor event in which 100 bonfires are lit in the water as haunting music is broadcast throughout the park. We all felt shivers down our spines watching the darkly clad figures light each fire in the middle of the canal.

The next day, Sunday, was proclaimed beach day by Emily, our youngest daughter. After scanning the map we chose Scarborough State Beach, a beautifully maintained facility on Rhode Island Sound that was only one hour from our hotel. The warm sand and the sound of waves induced a state of relaxation in all of us as we dozed, sunbathed, and read. We ended the day with a drive to Point Judith lighthouse, where we searched for seashells along the rocky shore and watched the ferry depart for Block Island.

Monday morning we drove back into downtown Providence to take a tour of Brown University. This was the school our rising senior, Caroline, wanted to see. In the same historic area of Providence we took a self-guided walking tour of Benefit Street's Mile of History, an impressive concentration of original colonial homes. We were amazed by the architectural details that have been so wonderfully preserved over the centuries. Seeking relief from the city heat, we hopped back in our van for a drive to Newport, famous for stately mansions, wonderful music festivals, and great sporting events. There we hiked along the famous Cliff Walk, a 3.5-mile trail along the Atlantic Ocean with views of many of the summer mansions.

On the drive home on Tuesday we started a list of the many activities we didn't have time to do. We're waiting for another vacation to sample the Roger Williams Park Zoo or the Newport Music Festival or maybe the tennis championships. And did I mention the wonderful Italian food in Providence?

The Theriault family, clockwise from top: Wayne, Caroline, Emily, Pat, and Nicole.

Nicole, Emily, and Caroline pose in front of Point Judith Head Light, one of many lighthouses along the 200-mile coastline of Rhode Island.

PARTICIPATE!

On the Road with Hampton™ wants to publish YOUR thoughts, observations, and ideas. So many of our guests have stories to tell about their travels and visits to Hampton hotels. We invite you to send us an article, not more than 750 words, describing a great road trip or vacation you've taken that included a stay at a Hampton Hotel or Hampton Inn & Suites. If your letter is chosen, you'll receive a FREE three-night stay at any Hampton Hotel. To enter, send your article to: *On the Road with Hampton*, 755 Crossover Lane, Memphis, TN 38117, or via e-mail to: ziba_rector@hilton.com. Please be sure to include a phone number.

Botanical Name *Rhoeo spathacea*
Local Name Purple Leaf Herb

Characteristics

This is a small herbaceous plant. It is fast growing and its leaves are green on top but pinkish purple underneath. Other species such as *Rhoeo discolor* can grow taller and are more attractive. The leaves can be boiled with rock sugar and make good delicious herbal Chinese tea. Its white small flowers are insignificant.

Height of Growth

The *Rhoeo spathacea* grows up to 30cm while the *Rhoeo discolor* can grow up to 60cm or so.

Recommended Planting Position

It is best for border planting and it gives added colour to other green plants. However, they should be weeded out when they grow too dense. They present better in semi-shade.

PALMS

Palms are often planted for their decorative features and elegant plant forms. They can create a pleasant and informal atmosphere which trees cannot. They are popular plants for shopfronts and courtyards of condominiums, apartments especially beside the swimming pools where partial shade is only required. But more importantly, palms are invariably chosen for their aesthetic qualities. By nature, the majority of palm species do not like full exposure to the sun. They revel in sheltered positions and grow well in semi-shaded localities in soils with good drainage and a high level of organic matter to sustain healthy growth. They are generally hardy subjects requiring fairly low maintenance.

Botanical Name *Chrysalidocarpus lutescens*
Local Name Yellow Cane Palm, Madagascar Palm

Characteristics
　　This palm has short trunks but the suckers from its base shoot out in a cluster of 8-9 trunks. The fronds are curved outwards and have yellow midribs. The centre stem is usually pale grey in colour.

Height of Growth
　　It can grow up to 4 metres high.

Recommended Planting Position
　　It can be planted at the end of a swimming pool or the pool deck, in restricted sites where it can be contained in planting troughs.

Botanical Name *Areca catechu*
Local Name   Pokok Pinang, Betel Nut Palm

Characteristics

This is a fast growing palm with a small and long trunk. It bears its fruits under the leaves from its trunk. Its leaves tend to arch and bend inwards. Its fruits are yellow to red in colour when ripe. Its kernel is eaten with "serih" leaves by early Malaysian ladies and workmen as a pastime delicacy.

Height of Growth

It can grow up to 20 metres high.

Recommended Planting Position

This palm is best planted in clusters to form a feature in large gardens, or in rows to form an avenue. It does not provide much shade.

Botanical Name *Borasus flabellifer*
Local Name Lontar, Palmyra Palm or Sea Coconut

Characteristics
This palm has a straight and upright trunk. It has a large crown of large leaves. The flowers and fruits are produced in bunches. The trunk is smooth and grey in colour. The kernel of the young fruits are soft and make delicious soft drinks. The fruits are flat at the two ends and are about 10cm oblong in shape. The tree is distinquishable by its round and thick crown.

Height of Growth
It can grow up to 20-25 metres high. A long lasting palm.

Recommended Planting Position
It is best planted in clusters in order to give good shade in large gardens, or park lands. It is not suitable for small gardens.

Botanical Name *Archontophoenix alexandrae*
Local Name King Palm, Alexandra Palm

Characteristics
This palm has a fairly large base and tapers to its centre stem. It has a fairly slender trunk and flowers at the stem level. It is native to Eastern Australia and its leaves are general longer than the Betel Nut Palm.

Height of Growth
It can grow up to 8 metres high or more depending on its age.

Recommended Planting Position
It can be grown in large gardens together with some flowering shrubs or in park lands.

Botanical Name *Cocos nucifera*
Local Name Coconut, Kelapa

Characteristics

It is a slow growing palm and can be graceful and attractive. Its leaves consist of long stalks up to 3 metres long and drooping. It bears its fruits between the stalks of the leaves. Some are yellow, green and reddish pink. Some dwarf species are grown for their beauty because of its ability to sway its trunk and leaves in the wind.

Height of Growth

Some coconut palms can grow up to 25 metres high, depending on the species.

Recommended Planting Position

The palm can be planted where semi-shade is required and gives an atmosphere of the seaside. It is best planted in clusters. It can also be planted along swimming pool decks, to give that tropical ambience.

Botanical Name *Cycas revoluta*
Local Name Cycad Palm

Characteristics

This is a very slow growing palm and can be planted in large pots or gardens. The leaflets are long and narrow with pointed ends. Its trunk is usually short unless it has aged for a long time. The crown is usually flared out into a diameter approximately 3 metres wide. There are two species found in Malaysia and they originate from Taiwan, or Northern Territory of Australia.

Height of Growth

The small plants are about 1.5 metres high and older plants can grow up to 3 metres or so.

Recommended Planting Position

It can be planted in large pots in full sun but for house gardens one must ensure that it should be kept out of reach of children, as its seeds are poisonous. Otherwise, it is a very attractive and decorative palm.

Botanical Name *Cyrtostachys lakka*
Local Name Pinang Rajah, Candle Wax Palm

Characteristics
This palm has a long and thin trunk and is pink to red at the top just below the leaves. It is a fairly fast growing palm and young shoots sprout out at its trunk base as the palm grows taller. It is grown mainly for its colourful trunk as a decorative feature in the garden.

Height of Growth
It can grow up to 18 metres high.

Recommended Planting Position
It can be planted in small gardens and at corners of a building as a feature or in parks or entrances leading to a porch. It can grow well in any soil and cannot withstand full sun. It prefers a semi-shaded position.

TROPICAL TREES AND SHRUBS PLANTING

Botanical Name *Lantania loddigesii*
Local Name Madagascar Palm

Characteristics

This is a slow growing palm. Its large leaves appear to be broken into many segments. The fronds radiate outwards very gracefully. The colour of its leaves is silvery green and shimmer in the sun. It can grow up to 10 metres high in open gardens.

Recommended Planting Position

It is recommended to plant in large gardens only as this species have very large leaf fronds and occupy space. It is not suitable to plant in planter boxes. Its attractiveness lies in the colour and form of its leaves. Colour is a beautiful bluish green.

Botanical Name *Latania lontaroides*
Local Name Golden Net Palm

Characteristics

This is a slow growing palm. Its broad fan-like leaves have a silvery shimmer in the bright sunlight. Latania palm has large fan-like leaves and radiate outwards occupying space. Its leaves are light green and the fruits are light grey and oval in shape. It can be distinguished easily by the colour of leaves and stalks.

Height of Growth

It can grow up to 12 metres high.

Recommended Planting Position

It is not suitable for small gardens and small plants should be planted in pots initially. It is good for large gardens and park lands.

Botanical Name *Livistona chinensis*
Local Name Pokok Serdang, Chinese Fan Palm

Characteristics

This palm has fan-shaped leaves which droop inwards towards the trunk. Its broad leaves usually are broken at the ends, giving a droopy appearance. It originated from Southern China hence the name Chinese Fan Palm. Its trunk is fairly short and squat. The leaves are usually light green in colour.

Height of Growth

It can grow up to 20 metres high.

Recommended Planting Position

It is a good ornamental palm and suitable to plant in a row as wind break and in park lands and large gardens. Ornamental only during the first 15 years or so.

Botanical Name   *Livistona rotundifolia*
Local Name   Serdang, Malayan Fan Palm

Characteristics
This palm has straight fan-like leaves which are not drooping. When young, the trunk is usually covered with brown husk but as it grows older the trunk becomes smooth and light grey in colour. Old fronds persist halfway down the trunk.

Height of Growth
This palm can grow up to 25 metres high and because of its thick crown it gives good shade.

Recommended Planting Position
It is suitable to plant in large gardens, road sides where reasonable shade is needed.

Botanical Name *Mascarena lagenicaulis*
Local Name Champagne Bottle Palm

Characteristics

This is a slow growing palm. The base of the trunk is enlarged as it grows older and taller. It gradually forms the shape of a champagne bottle and that is where it gets its name but will lose this characteristic shape as it grows older. The leaves are strong and stiff on long stalks spreading out from its central trunk.

Height of Growth

It can grow up to 2 metres or so in open gardens.

Recommended Planting Position

As it is a clean and neat palm, it is suitable to plant it in the garden in clusters and supported by some colourful groundcovers or by the roadside.

Botanical Name *Ptychosperma macarthurii*
Local Name Macarthur Palm

Characteristics

This palm is fairly fast growing and like any other palms, its flowers and fruits are grown under the leaves. It is easily recognised by its spreading trunks or shoots from the base, usually in fours or more. The trunks are not more than 10cm in diameter and are dark green in colour. Its appearance is best when the young shoots are not extracted from the mother plant at the base. The hanging bright red fruits are attractive against its dark green leaves.

Height of Growth

It can grow up to 5 metres high when it is fully matured. It looks its best at the height of 3 metres.

Recommended Planting Position

These palms are best planted with other groundcovers so that they do not appear bare at the base of its trunks. It can be planted by the roadside, in house gardens and park lands. Grows best in sheltered positions.

Botanical Name *Rhapis excelsa*
Local Name Lady Palm

Characteristics

A very slow growing and graceful palm species, rather dwarf bamboo-like stems arising from rootstock bearing that open out like miniature fans. The stems are very strong and much sought after for building bird cages and walking-sticks. This palm, like all other palms, revels in good well-drained soil which is high in organic content. It grows in a clump habit arising from the basal rootstock.

Height of Growth

It has a dwarf habit of growth, growing to a maximum of 2 metres or more in low light areas. It is very ornamental in containers.

Recommended Planting Position

It prefers semi-shade and can withstand low light intensities. Very useful for indoor decoration and needs to be rotated after certain period. Ideal for courtyard or patio planting. Good as a low screen in bed planting in shady gardens.

Botanical Name *Roystonea oleracca*
Local Name Cabbage Palm

Characteristics

This palm has a large base trunk like that of *Roystonea regia* and it tapers upwards to its stem. It is reasonably big on the average of 50 to 80cm. Its spreading leaves are similar to Betel Nut Palm and are dark green in colour. Its trunk is smooth, marked by rings of fallen leaves. It originated from the West Indies and South America.

Height of Growth

It can grow up to 40 metres in the open.

Recommended Planting Position

Because of its clear appearance, it can be planted by the poolside deck, or along the foot path of condominium apartments and offices. It is a much cleaner palm than the *Roystonea regia*.

Botanical Name *Roystonea regia*
Local Name Royal Palm

Characteristics
This is a fast growing palm with white greyish trunk. The trunk usually appears to be swollen near the basal portion and tapers towards its leaves at the top. It can be recognised by its elegant, clean and long trunk punctuated only by the scar rings of past fallen leaves. The leaves are dark green in colour and broken into a series of leaflets which do not provide good shade under the sun. It originated from Cuba.

Height of Growth
It can grow up to 40 metres.

Recommended Planting Position
It is suitable to plant in a colonade or in rows at 10 metres apart to mark an avenue of grandeur in large gardens or park lands.

TREES

Page	Botanical Names	Local Names	Maximum Height	Recommended Planting Position	Caution
1	*Acacia auriculiformis*	Wattle, Yellow Acacia	45 metres	Full Sun, PL, RS, LG	Branches liable to break in strong wind
2	*Acacia mangium*	Broadleaf Acacia	20 metres	Full Sun, LG, WB, gives good shade	
3	*Alstonia angustiloba*	Pokok Pulai	60 metres	Full Sun, LG, PL	Roots can damage any pavement
4	*Araucaria excelsa*	Norfolk Pine	40 metres	LG, PL	
5	*Bauhinia blakeana*	Butterfly Tree	7-10 metres	SG, Eastern aspect not exposed to hot afternoon sun	Fast growing with fairly large leaves, provides light shade
6	*Casuarina nobile*	Pokok Ru Roneng	15 metres	SG, PL, RS, Western aspect	
7	*Cerbera odollam*	Pong-Pong Tree	12 metres	Full Sun, LG	Leaves drop during dry weather, poisonous fruits
8	*Cinnamomum iners*	Wild Cinnamon, Medang Teja, Pokok Manis	15 metres	SG, Good screen, Gives good shade	Should be planted 3 metres apart
9	*Cyathea* spp	Lowland Tree Fern	4 metres	Semi-shade, Near water and rocks	Tough fibrous trunk
10	*Delonix regia*	Semarak Api, Flame of the Forest	18 metres	LG, Full Sun, Flowers well in dry weather	Slow growing, deciduous
11	*Erythrina glauca*	Pokok Dedap	15 metres	Full Sun, Western aspect, gives good shade	Deciduous, quick growing
12	*Erythrina variegata*	Variegated Coral Tree, Pokok Dedap, Dedap Batik	15 metres	LG, RS, gives good shade	Fast growing, spiny twigs
13	*Ficus maclellandi*	Long Leaf Ficus	10 metres	LG, gives good shade	Spreading roots, fast growing, not subject to insect attack.
14	*Ficus varigata*	Golden Leaves	5 metres	Full Sun, PA	Look best below 1.5 metres.
15	*Filicium decipiens*	Fern leaved tree	20 metres	LG, RS, PL, gives good shade	Fast growing, spreading foliage
16	*Fragraea fragrans*	Pokok Tembusu	30 metres	Full Sun, LG, WB	Gives semi-shade, slow growing
17	*Michelia alba*	Chempaka Putih	21 metres	Full Sun, LG, RS	Gives good shade
18	*Mimusops elengi*	Bunga Tanjung	20 metres	RS, LG, gives good shade	Fast growing, sandy soil, little maintenance
19	*Peltophorum pterocarpum*	Yellow Flame, Batai Laut, Jemerlang	45 metres	LG, PL, gives good shade	Deciduous, dense foliage
20	*Persea americana*	Avocado Pear Tree	20 metres	LG, western aspect, gives good shade	Fast growing,
21	*Pithecellobium dulce*	Madras Thorn	15 metres	LG, PL, RS	Fast growing, Thorny branches
22	*Plumeria acuminata*	Frangipani	5-6 metres	LG, PL, RS, gives reasonable shade	Stout tree with strong trunk, can withstand very dry soil condition
23	*Polyalthia longifolia*	Mast Tree	15 metres	LG, PL	Fast growing
24	*Pterocarpus indicus*	Angsana, Sena	30 metres	PL, RS, LG	Fast growing, becomes straggly if not pruned
25	*Ravenala magascariensis*	Traveller's Palm	20 metres	SG, PL, sheltered position	Loses its majestic appearance if grows too high, fast growing
26	*Sterculia foetida*	Pokok Kelumpang	35 metres	LG, PL, RS, gives reasonable shade	Fast growing, deciduous
27	*Syzgium malaccense*	Jambu Bol	20 metres	LG, gives good shade, western aspect	Can withstand dry condition, fast growing

LG—large garden SG—small garden PA—pool area PL—park land RS—roadside (shoulder) WB—windbreak

SHRUBS

Page	Botanical Names	Local Names	Maximum Height	Recommended Planting Position	Caution
29	*Acalypha siamensis*	Siamese Acalypha, Tea Leaves	1.2 metres	Full Sun, well-drained soil, Planting distance is 30cm apart	Fast growing
30	*Acalypha wilkinsiana*	Acalypha (Red Leaf Type) or Hawaiian Acalypha	2-3 metres	Hedging	Looks well against white background
31	*Acalypha wilkinsiana*	Acalypha (Yellow green Variegated type)	2-3 metres	Hedging	Looks well against white background
32	*Allamanda cathartica*	Yellow Bells	1.5 metres	Large pots	Continuous flowering
33	*Averrhoa bilimbi*	Bilimbing Asam	6 metres	Full Sun, well-drained soil	gives good shade
34	*Bambusa nana*	Hedge Bamboo, Bamboo Pagar	4 metres	Hedging	Fast growing, constant trimming
35	*Bougainvillea*	Bunga Kertas, Mary Palmer Bougainvillea	15 metres	Full sun exposure for planters and open garden	Constant pruning and manuring
36	*Bougainvillea glabra variegata*	Variegated Bougainvillea	15 metres	Full Sun, planter box	Does not flower well
37	*Bougainvillea spectabilis*	Golden Bougainvillea, Variegated Bougainvillea	15 metres	Full Sun, sandy soil	Constant pruning, can become a creeper
38	*Caesalpinia pulcherrima*	Peacock Flower, Pride of Barbados	5 metres	Full Sun, tolerates poor soil	Minimum maintenance, prune to keep in good shape
39	*Callistemon lanceolatus*	Bottle Brush	8 metres	Well-drained soil, PL	Slow growing, attracts small birds, fairly dense foliage
40	*Cassia spectabilis*	Scented Cassia	6 metres	LG, well-drained soil	semi-shade
41	*Cassia surattensis*	Glaucous Cassia	4 metres	LG, semi-shade, well-drained soil	Fast growing, becomes very straggly and untidy
42	*Codiaeum puntatum aureum*	Golden dwarf codiaeum	30-45cm	Full Sun, mass planting, pot specimens	dense and bushy plant
43	*Cordyline terminalis*	Red Edge	3 metres	Full Sun, grow in cluster, suitable for planter box	Slender trunks
44	*Cythula prostrata*	Cythula Groundcover	60cm	Good groundcover	Fast growing creeper
45	*Dracaena marginata*	Rainbow Fern	5 metres	Full Sun, planter box, ideal pot plant	Slow growing
46	*Ficus benjamina variegata*	Variegated Ficus	3 metres	Full Sun, planter box	
47	*Ficus nitida variegata*	Golden-Leaved Ficus	3 metres	Full Sun, hedging	
48	*Hibiscus rosa sinensis*	Hibiscus, Bunga Raya	3 metres	Full Sun, RS, SG, hedging	
49	*Hibiscus rosa sinensis (Cooperi)*	Cotton Leaf Hibiscus	2 metres	Full Sun, hedging	Seldom bears flowers
50	*Hibiscus rosa sinensis (crested)*	Chicken Crest Hibiscus	2 metres	Full Sun	well-drained soil
51	*Ixora "sunkiss"*	Small Siantan		Full Sun, well-drained soil, grow in cluster	Very free flowering
52	*Ixora chinensis*	Ixora	1.2 metres	Full Sun, well-drained soil	Blooms well after pruning and application of fertiliser
53	*Ixora coccinea (yellow)*	Yellow Ixora	1.2 metres	Full Sun, well-drained soil, plant-box	High moisture level in the soil
54	*Lagerstroemia indica*	Inai Merah, Crepe Myrtle	1.2 metres	Full Sun and opening space	Fast growing, needs regular pruning to flower well
55	*Lantana montevidensis*	Bunga Misi		Full Sun, well-drained soil, large planter box	Creeper with thorny stems and branches

LG–large garden   SG–small garden   PA–pool area   PL–park land   RS–roadside (shoulder)   WB–windbreak

Page	Botanical Names	Local Names	Maximum Height	Recommended Planting Position	Caution
56	Lochnera rosea (Vinca rosea Catharanthus rosea)	Periwinkle, Kemunting Cina	1 metre	Full Sun, well-drained soil, as border plants, grow in clusters	Flowers bloom at top of leaf axils
57	Pandanus pygmaeus	Golden Pygmy		Full Sun/semi-shade, edging strip	Spreads as a groundcover fast, needs constant watering
58	Phyllanthus myrtifolius	Phyllanthus, Mouse Tail Plant		Full Sun, planters, good border plants	Regular application of fertilisers, leaves are partially closed or folded at night
59	Pisonia alba	Mengkudu Siani, Lettuce Tree	8 metres	Full Sun, gives good shade, LG, PL	
60	Plumbago capensis	Plumbago Blue	20cm	Full Sun but grow best in sheltered position, wet soil condition, planter box	border plant
61	Polyscias filicifolia	Golden Polyscias	1.2 metres	Full Sun, hedging	
62	Pseudoeranthemum reticulatum	Golden Leaves Flower	40-50cm	Full Sun, sandy soil, border plant	Small flowers
63	Rhoeo spathacea	Purple Leaf Herb	30cm	Semi-shade, border plant	Needs weeding when grows too dense

PALMS

Page	Botanical Names	Local Names	Maximum Height	Recommended Planting Position	Caution
65	Archontophoenix alexandrae	King Palm, Alexandra Palm	8 metres	Full Sun, LG, PL	Fairly large base
66	Areca catechu	Pokok Pinang, Betel Nut Palm	20 metres	Full Sun, LG, plant in rows	Does not provide much shade,
67	Borasus flabellifer	Lontar, Palmyra Palm or Sea Coconut	20-25 metres	Full Sun, LG, PL, gives good shade	A long lasting palm
68	Chrysalidocarpus lutescens	Yellow Cane Palm, Madagascar Palm	4 metres	Full Sun, PA	Can be contained in planting troughs
69	Cocos nucifera	Coconut, Kelapa	25 metres	Full Sun, gives semi-shade	Gives an atmosphere of seaside, slow growing
70	Cycas revoluta	Cycad Palm	3 metres	Full Sun, large pot	Slow growing, poisonous seeds
71	Cyrtostachys lakka	Pinang Rajah, Candle Wax Palm	18 metres	Semi-shade, any soil	Fairly fast growing
72	Lantania loddigesii	Madagascar Palm	10 metres	Full Sun, not suitable for planter box	Slow growing
73	Latania lontaroides	Golden Net Palm	12 metres	Full Sun, LG, PL	Slow growing
74	Livistona chinensis	Pokok Serdang, Chinese Fan Palm	20 metres	Full Sun, LG, PL	Ornamental only during first 15 years or so
75	Livistona rotundifolia	Serdang, Malayan Fan Palm	25 metres	Full Sun, LG, RS	Old fonds persist halfway down the trunk
76	Mascarena lagenicaulis	Champagne Bottle Palm	2 metres	Full Sun, SG, RS	Lose shape as it grows older
77	Ptychosperma macarthurii	Macarthur Palm	5 metres	Sheltered position, RS, SG, PL	Fast growing
78	Rhapis excelsa	Lady Palm		Can withstand low light, well-drained soil high in organic content, useful for indoor decoration, patio, low screen	Very slow growing
79	Roystonea oleracca	Cabbage Palm	40 metres	Full Sun, PA, LG	Large base trunk
80	Roystonea regia	Royal Palm	40 metres	Full Sun, LG, PL	Fast growing

LG–large garden   SG–small garden   PA–pool area   PL–park land   RS–roadside (shoulder)   WB–windbreak

INDEX

Acacia auriculiformis	1	Chempaka Putih	17	Ixora	52
Acacia cicinnata	1	Chicken Crest Hibiscus	50	*Ixora "sunkiss"*	51
Acacia mangium	2	Chinese Fan Palm	74	*Ixora chinensis*	52
Acalypha (Red Leaf Type)	30	*Chrysalidocarpus lutescens*	68	*Ixora coccinea* (yellow)	53
Acalypha (Yellow Green Variegated type)	31	*Cinnamomum iners*	8	Jambu Bol	27
		Coconut	69	Jemerlang	19
Acalypha siamensis	29	*Cocos nucifera*	69	*jermes inoplenus*	48
Acalypha wilkinsiana	30	*Codiaeum puntatum aureum*	42	Kelapa	69
Acalypha wilkinsiana	31	*Cordyline terminalis*	43	Kemunting Cina	56
Alexandra Palm	65	*Cotton Leaf Hibiscus*	49	King Palm	65
Allamanda cathartica	32	Crepe Myrtle	54	Lady Palm	78
Allamanda schottii	32	*Cyathea spp*	9	*Lagerstroemia indica*	54
Alstonia angustiloba	3	Cycad Palm	70	*Lantana montevidensis*	55
Angsana	24	*Cycas revoluta*	70	*Lantania loddigesii*	72
Araucaria excelsa	4	*Cyrtostachys lakka*	71	*Latania lontaroides*	73
Archontophoenix alexandrae	65	Cythula Groundcover	44	Lateritic Gold	35
Areca catechu	66	*Cythula prostrata*	44	Lettuce Tree	59
Averrhoa bilimbi	33	Dedap Batik	12	*Livistona chinensis*	74
Avocado Pear Tree	20	*Delonix regia*	10	*Livistona rotundifolia*	75
Bamboo Pagar	34	*Dracaena marginata*	45	*Lochnera rosea*	56
Bambusa nana	34	*Dracaena marginata* (Tricolor)	45	*Lochnera rosea* var *alba*	56
Batai Laut	19	*Erythrina glauca*	11	Long Leaf Ficus	13
Bauhinia blakeana	5	*Erythrina variegata*	12	Lontar	67
Betel Nut Palm	65, 66, 79	Fern leaved tree	15	Lowland Tree Fern	9
Bilimbing Asam	33	*Ficus benjamina variegata*	46	Macarthur Palm	77
Borasus flabellifer	67	*Ficus maclellandi*	13	Madagascar Palm	68
Bottle Brush	39	*Ficus nitida variegata*	47	Madagascar Palm	72
Bougainvillea buttiana "Mrs Butt"	35	*Ficus varigata*	14	Madras Thorn	21
		Filicium decipiens	15	Malayan Fan Palm	75
Bougainvillea glabra variegata	36	Flame of the Forest	10	Mary Palmer Bougainvillea	35
Bougainvillea spectabilis	35, 37	*Fragraea fragrans*	16	*Mascarena lagenicaulis*	76
Bougainvillea	35	Frangipani	22	Mast Tree	23
Broadleaf Acacia	2	Glaucous Cassia	41	Medang Teja	8
Bunga Kertas	35	Golden Bougainvillea	37	Mengkudu Siani	59
Bunga Misi	55	Golden dwarf codiaeum	42	*Michelia alba*	17
Bunga Raya	48	Golden Leaves	14	*Mimusops elengi*	18
Bunga Tanjung	18	Golden Leaves Flower	62	Mouse Tail Plant	58
Butterfly Tree	5	Golden Net Palm	73	Norfolk Pine	4
Cabbage Palm	79	Golden Polyscias	61	Palmyra Palm	67
Caesalpinia pulcherrima	38	Golden Pygmy	57	*Pandanus pygmaeus*	57
Callistemon lanceolatus	39	Golden-Leaved Ficus	47	Peacock Flower	38
Candle Wax Palm	71	Hawaiian Acalypha	30	*Peltophorum pterocarpum*	19
Cassia spectabilis	40	Hedge Bamboo	34	Periwinkle	56
Cassia surattensis	41	Hibiscus	48	*Persea americana*	20
Casuarina nobile	6	*Hibiscus rosa sinensis* (*Cooperi*)	49	Phyllanthus	58
Catharanthus rosea	56	*Hibiscus rosa sinensis* (*crested*)	50	*Phyllanthus myrtifolius*	58
Cerbera odollam	7	*Hibiscus rosa sinensis*	48	Pinang Rajah	71
Champagne Bottle Palm	76	Inai Merah	54	*Pisonia alba*	59

Pithecellobium dulce	21	Pong-Pong Tree	7	Siamese Acalypha	29
Plumbago Blue	60	Pride of Barbados	38	Small Siantan	51
Plumbago capensis	60	*Pseudoeranthemum reticulatum*	62	*Sterculia foetida*	26
Plumeria acuminata	22	*Pterocarpus indicus*	24	*Syzgium malaccense*	27
Plumeria obtusa	22	*Ptychosperma macarthurii*	77	Tea Leaves	29
Plumeria rubra	22	Purple Leaf Herb	63	Traveller's Palm	25
Pokok Dedap	11	Rainbow Fern	45	Variegated Bougainvillea	36
Pokok Dedap	12	*Ravenala magascariensis*	25	Variegated Bougainvillea	37
Pokok Kelumpang	26	Red Edge	43	Variegated Coral Tree	12
Pokok Manis	8	*Rhapis excelsa*	78	Variegated Ficus	46
Pokok Pinang	66	*Rhoeo spathacea*	63	*Vinca rosea*	56
Pokok Pulai	3	*Rhoeo discolor*	63	Wattle	1
Pokok Ru Roneng	6	Royal Palm	80	Wild Cinnamon	8
Pokok Serdang	74	*Roystonea oleracca*	79	Yellow Acacia	1
Pokok Tembusu	16	*Roystonea regia*	79, 80	Yellow Bells	32
Polyalthia longifolia	23	Sabah Acacia	1	Yellow Cane Palm	68
Polyscias filicifolia	61	Scented Cassia	40	Yellow Flame	19
Polyscias balfouriana (Maginata)	61	Sea Coconut	67	Yellow Ixora	53
		Semarak Api	10		
Polyscias quilfoylee (Quinquefolia)	61	Sena	24		
		Serdang	75		

References

1. Selected Plants and Planting for a Garden City
   (forty popular climbers)
   by The Ministry of Law and National Development Singapore

2. Selected Plants for Town and Country Beautification in Sarawak
   by Dr Paul P.K. Chai & Sylvester S.L. Liew

3. *Malaysian Trees in Colour*
   by Chin Hoong Fong

4. *Some Common Trees of Malaysia and Singapore*
   by Betty Molesworth Allen

5. *Pokok-Pokok untuk Taman Bandar*
   by Adnan Mohamed

6. *The Illustrated Ornamental Plants of Taiwan*